Gardener's Hints & Tips

Gardener's Hints & Tips

Antony Atha

This edition is published by Lorenz Books, an imprint of Anness Publishing Ltd,
Hermes House, 88–89 Blackfriars Road, London SE1 8HA; tel. 020 7401 2077; fax 020 7633 9499
www.lorenzbooks.com; www.annesspublishing.com

UK agent/distributor: Book Trade Services; tel. 0116 2759086; fax 0116 2759090;
uksales@booktradeservices.com; exportsales@booktradeservices.com
North American agent/distributor: National Book Network; tel. 301 459 3366; fax 301 429 5746; www.nbnbooks.com
Australian agent/distributor: Pan Macmillan Australia; tel. 1300 135 113; fax 1300 135 103; customer.service@macmillan.com.au
New Zealand agent/distributor: David Bateman Ltd; tel. (09) 415 7664; fax (09) 415 8892

If you like the images in this book and would like to investigate using them for publishing, promotions or advertising, please visit our website www.practicalpictures.com for more information.

Publisher: Joanna Lorenz
Project Editor: Joanne Rippin
Designer: Andrew Heath

ETHICAL TRADING POLICY
Because of our ongoing ecological investment programme, you, as our customer, can have the pleasure and reassurance of knowing that a tree is being cultivated on your behalf to naturally replace the materials used to make the book you are holding. For further information about this scheme, go to www.annesspublishing.com/trees

PUBLISHER'S NOTE
Although the advice and information in this book are believed to be accurate and true at the time of going to press, neither the authors nor the publisher can accept any legal responsibility or liability for any errors or omissions that may be made nor for any inaccuracies nor for any harm or injury that comes about from following instructions or advice in this book.

Contents

SPRING

Fresh spring the herald of love's mighty king,
In whose coat armour richly are display'd
All sorts of flowers the which on earth do spring
In goodly colours gloriously array'd.
(Edmund Spenser Amoretti "Sonnet LXX")

EARLY SPRING

THE FLOWER GARDEN

The first flowers of spring are one of the main delights of the gardener's year, particularly the early bulbs, winter aconites, snowdrops and early crocuses.

CARE & PROPAGATION

- Clear the lawn of sticks and sweep up any litter left by the winter storms.
- Mow the grass with the cutter blades set high if the weather is fine and dry.
- Tidy up any broken branches on trees or shrubs battered by winter gales. Trim ragged edges and paint with fungicide.
- Prune large-flowered clematis varieties (groups 1 and 3) down to 45 cm (18 in) from the ground.
- Prune wisteria: cut lateral shoots back to 2–3 buds.
- Prune rambling and shrub roses if required.
- Prune hybrid tea and floribunda roses if this has not been done before.
- Prune buddleia, *Hydrangea paniculata*, spirea, *Ceanothus* "Gloire de Versailles", ceratostigma, fuchsia, perovskia, romneya and cornus.
- Trim privet and hawthorn hedges.
- Trim winter-flowering heathers with shears to keep them tidy when they have finished flowering.

Above: A sun-drenched bed of crocuses making a stunning spring-time show.

Above: A mixture of delicate white snowdrops and yellow crocuses, flowers which are among the first signs of spring.

SOWING & PLANTING

- Divide herbaceous plants if the soil conditions permit and fill in any gaps in the border.
- Plant gladioli, galtonia and lily bulbs if this has not been done earlier.
- Sow sweet peas outside in a cold frame.
- Plan where to plant additional bulbs if these are required.
- Lift and separate snowdrops when flowering has finished as this encourages them to spread.

Top: Remember to dead-head your flowers as they die off, it will help your display to stay pretty for longer, but don't lift the bulbs until the leaves have died.

Above: White flowers always help to emphasize the colours of other plants. Here this pretty border spills over the bed on to the garden path.

Left: Old-fashioned buckets and watering cans can often be found in junk shops and add a distinct and attractive quality to most gardens, particularly modern ones.

Above: A lovely cherry tree in full blossom, one of the most distinctive signs of spring with its clusters of blush-pink flowers.

Hints & Tips

- Group 1 clematis are the ones which flower in the summer and autumn on new growth made in that year. Among these are *Clematis tangutica*, the *texensis* hybrids, the *viticella* varieties (which often have "v" after the name on the labels) and the large-flowered x *jackmanii* hybrids. Group 3 are the large-flowered varieties which flower from May through to July; "Nelly Moser" and "Lasurstern" are two very well-known varieties. Technically, these should be pruned more lightly or not at all, but if you don't prune them they quickly become straggly and unsightly.
- The best way to prune hybrid tea and floribunda roses is to cut them off regardless of buds and shoots 30 cm (12 in) above the ground. They will produce more flowers, although they look a bit untidy until they start to shoot. This is heresy to traditional gardeners.
- Let the foliage of all bulbs die down naturally – don't be tempted to mow the grass around them as this weakens the bulb, which may then be "blind" the following year.
- Don't be tempted to do too much work on the herbaceous borders as nature has a frost or two left to come.
- Keep the garden tidy and clear up any fallen branches and twigs.

THE KITCHEN GARDEN

Work in the kitchen garden at this time of year depends on the weather and your soil, because if it's cold and wet then little useful can be achieved.

CARE & PROPAGATION

- Cut out old raspberry canes (vines) if this has not been done in the previous autumn. Tie in the new canes (vines), allowing four to five per plant.
- Cut autumn-fruiting raspberries down to 15 cm (6 in) from the ground.
- Tidy up the strawberry bed, clear away any remaining runners and plant out a new bed if required.
- Spray fruit trees with a tar oil wash or copper-based fungicide.

SOWING & PLANTING

- Put clean polythene over the ground to help the soil warm up.
- When weather conditions permit, dig or rotavate the soil and prepare the bed for sowing.
- Sow broad beans (fava beans) if they were not sown in late autumn.
- Sow parsnips and early peas.
- Sow early shallots, Jerusalem artichokes and horseradish.
- Plant outdoor vines.
- Prepare cloches and sow early carrots and lettuce under them.
- Lift and separate old clumps of rhubarb and plant new crowns.

If disaster strikes, and for some reason your seedlings fail to thrive, you can always fall back on your local garden centre or commercial greenhouse for replacement plants.

Hints & Tips

- Early spring is a good time to tidy up the compost heap.
- Do not let your young strawberry plants fruit in their first year.
- Buy seeds and summer-flowering bulbs and throw away any seeds left over from last year.
- Make certain that all your machines are in working order and arrange to have mowers, cultivators and any other machines you may have serviced.

THE GREENHOUSE

The greenhouse can be a refuge at this time of year if there is frost and snow lingering. Many jobs can be done preparing and sowing seeds of flowers and vegetables.

Whatever its previous use may have been, a water butt to collect rainwater for use during dry summer months is an excellent idea.

- If you have potted-on bedding plants from the previous year, now is the time to take cuttings. This also applies to pelargoniums and chrysanthemums.
- Sow summer annuals: antirrhinum, marguerite, carnation, stocks, phlox, tobacco plant (nicotiana) and lobelia.
- Start tuberous begonias into growth in boxes of sandy soil.
- Sow seeds of hardy border perennials and rock plants such as dianthus (pinks), delphinium, lupin, bellflower (campanula), flax and geums.
- Repot any orchid plants that have become congested, using orchid compost (potting soil).

MID SPRING

THE FLOWER GARDEN

Spring sunshine is reflected in the yellow of the daffodils and forsythia. Many of the spring shrubs are now at their best, especially the magnolias and flowering cherries.

CARE & PROPAGATION

- Start mowing the lawn regularly and gradually reduce the height of the cutting blades. Apply selective weedkiller and fertilizer to the grass.
- Prune winter-flowering shrubs when they have finished flowering, such as winter jasmine (*Jasminum nudiflorum*) and wintersweet (*Chimonanthus praecox*).
- Trim winter-flowering heathers.
- Prune clematis and roses if this has not been done earlier.
- Cut back St John's wort (*Hypericum calycinum*).
- Trim ivy.
- Prune autumn-flowering ceanothus.
- Feed and mulch roses and all shrubs and hedges.
- Weed the herbaceous border, give it its final tidy (clean up) and then apply food and mulch.
- Start staking herbaceous plants.
- Take root cuttings of delphiniums.

Above: The weather may still be unsettled at this time of year, but the sight of trees in blossom gladdens the heart and heralds the coming of spring.

Right: A grassy path leading out of a pretty cottage garden. Difficult to maintain if there is plenty of coming and going, but it does make a lovely sight.

Sowing & Planting

- If you are planning a new lawn, prepare the site thoroughly and sow grass seed or lay new turf.
- Sow hardy annuals.
- Plant new perennials and shrubs.
- Plant out pot-sown sweet peas, summer bulbs and tubers, gladioli, crocosmia, lilies and galtonias.
- Plant ranunculus tubers.

Above: A sunken garden in the grounds of a large country house wtih iberis and aubrieta tumbling down the wall. These plants grow particularly well in a south-facing situation.

Top: Daffodils and hyacinths cut for a flower arrangement. It is a good idea to put the stems of all bulbs in water as soon as possible after cutting for the house.

Some gardens may have room for an elegant summerhouse such as this, here framed by wild woodland and flowering rhododendrons.

Hints & Tips

- Try to keep up to date with all the jobs that have to be done, but remember that many seeds can be sown later and planting can be postponed especially if the weather turns cold.
- This is a good time of the year to sow a new lawn or prepare and plant a new herbaceous border. In both cases the site should be well prepared, and it is worth reading a good instructional book before starting either task.
- Soil temperature should be a minimum of 7°C (45°F) for seeds to germinate, so don't sow your new lawn until the soil reaches this temperature.
- Don't use weedkiller on new lawns until they are properly established.
- Brush the lawn with sand if your garden is on heavy clay and you want to improve the drainage.
- Start applying selective weedkillers to perennial weeds and remember that you can get rid of many weeds by mowing or hoeing them constantly throughout the year.
- When weeding keep all perennial weeds separate from other garden refuse and do not put them on your compost heap.
- Dead-head daffodils and narcissus when they finish flowering, to conserve the strength of the bulbs, and feed the foliage with liquid fertilizer.
- Mark clumps of bulbs which seem overcrowded and dig up and split (divide) them later in the summer or when the foliage has died down.

THE KITCHEN GARDEN

As the days get longer and the soil warms up you can start to plant the kitchen garden. Plan your planting carefully and protect young plants from the birds.

Planting out Seedlings

1 Always prepare your soil properly before planting. Rake the seed beds to a fine tilth.

2 It is a good idea to grow brassicas in individual modules. Water, then remove by pushing gently from the bottom.

3 Space the plants out according to the instructions on the seed packet. Firm the soil around the plant and water.

- Plant new fruit trees and bushes as early as possible.
- Weed and mulch fruit bushes and strawberry beds.
- Dig or rotavate the soil to break it down into prepared beds.
- Plant asparagus crowns.
- Start sowing vegetables.
- Plant potatoes. Traditionally these were planted on Good Friday in the Northern Hemisphere.
- Protect plants from frost and birds with garden fleece (netting).

A bluebell border lines the path in this English country garden.

Hints & Tips

- In dry spells keep newly planted fruit bushes well-watered to encourage the formation of good roots before the dry weather sets in.
- Make a chart of where you plan to sow your vegetables, and remember to rotate potatoes and brassicas (cabbages, kales) in your kitchen garden.
- Sow carrots, peas and lettuces at fortnightly (biweekly) intervals throughout the summer for a succession of young plants.

THE GREENHOUSE

Greenhouses in mid spring are wonderful places, with seedlings and young plants bursting with life, growth and vitality.

A large country garden greenhouse growing young plants on a scale unlikely to be matched in any domestic garden.

- Sow outdoor tomatoes, runner beans (string beans) and cucumbers to plant out later.
- Take dahlia cuttings.
- Pot up pelargonium and fuchsia cuttings.
- Start begonia and gloxinia tubers into growth.
- Sow seeds of bedding and pot plants and prick out (thin out) any seedlings that were sown earlier.
- Sow tender vegetables such as marrows (squash), courgettes (zucchini) and sweetcorn (corn).
- Take leaf cuttings of saintpaulias and streptocarpus.

LATE SPRING

THE FLOWER GARDEN

As the days lengthen, apple and pear blossom makes one of the most beautiful sights of the year, and colour returns to the herbaceous border.

CARE & PROPAGATION

- Treat the lawn with selective weed-killer if necessary and liquid fertilizer.
- Prune early-flowering shrubs after flowering. These plants flower on the wood made the previous year and it is necessary to give them a long growing season. They include forsythia, syringa (lilac), weigela, philadelphus and berberis.
- Feed roses and spray if signs of greenfly, black spot or mildew appear.
- Take softwood cuttings of shrubs such as, caryopteris, forsythia, fuchsia, kolkwitzia and salvia.
- Continue to stake herbaceous plants.
- Harden off tender bedding plants.
- Cut back plants in the rock garden when they finish flowering to keep them tidy.
- Dig up primulas when they have finished flowering. Divide up the clumps and replant, adding a small amount of fertilizer to the soil.
- Take cuttings of nepeta (catmint) and dianthus (pinks).
- Clear spring flower beds.
- Lift tulip bulbs after flowering when the foliage has died down.
- Water all lime-hating plants with a foliar feed containing chelated iron.

SOWING & PLANTING

- Fill in any gaps in the herbaceous border with container grown plants.
- Plant up the water garden if you have one and divide any pond plants that have become too large.
- Sow sweet peas out of doors.
- Sow hardy annuals, especially godetia, love-in-a-mist, alyssum, flax, clarkia and candytuft.
- Plant out half-hardy annuals raised from seed under glass: stocks, asters, marigolds and nemesia.
- Sow hardy biennials, such as wall-flowers, sweet williams, canterbury bells, foxgloves and honesty, out of doors.
- Sow seeds of hardy perennials: hollyhocks, gaillardia, dianthus (pinks), lupins and delphiniums.
- Sow seeds of rock garden plants you want to add to your rockery.
- Plant out dahlia tubers.
- Plant up window-boxes, containers and hanging baskets.
- At the end of the period, when all danger from frost has passed, start planting out summer bedding plants.
- Finish planting out gladioli and summer bulbs.

Above: Pretty pots of flowers grace the late spring garden.

Planting a Shrub

1 First dig a large enough hole and add compost. Water the shrub and leave for an hour. Tease out some of the roots to encourage them to grow into new soil.

2 Use your feet to make sure that the soil is firmly pressed around the plant, then water again.

Above: A medium-sized town garden is used to maximum effect with an impressive visual display of beds. A garden shed has its harsh walls softened by a trellis and the patio in the foreground is edged with pots of flowers.

Hints & Tips

- It is difficult to spread granular fertilizers or weed-killers evenly on a lawn without a properly designed spreader. These can usually be hired (rented). Mark off the lawn carefully to ensure that the correct amount is applied and water the lawn if it has not rained within two to three days after application.
- Prevention is better than cure and a programme of spraying roses every two weeks against greenfly, mildew and black spot is recommended. There are a number of good commercial sprays available which do not harm birds or beneficial insects.
- Aubrietia, *Gypsophila repens*, flax, saponaria, edelweiss and dwarf geraniums can all be raised from seed for the rock garden.
- Watch gardeners in the local parks and don't put your bedding plants out until they do.
- Label tulip bulbs when you lift them, store them carefully and replant in the autumn. You can leave them in place but if you do, give them a good foliar feed to build up their strength.
- Mulch around shrubs and newly planted trees.

THE KITCHEN GARDEN

This is one of the busiest times of the year in the kitchen garden, but be careful of late frosts and delay planting if these threaten.

CARE & PROPAGATION

- Check that all the raspberry canes (vines) are in position and tied in.
- Put straw around strawberry plants and mulch them.
- Mulch fruit trees.
- Spray apple trees when the blossom has fallen to keep off pests such as caterpillars.
- Take softwood cuttings of black-currant bushes.
- Prepare netting to keep birds off fruit bushes, or make a fruit cage if necessary.
- If a frost threatens protect early potatoes with a plastic cover.
- Earth up potatoes.

Above: An immaculate kitchen garden. Plant sweetcorn (corn) in a group for successful fertilization.

Above: Broad beans (fava beans) are now well advanced. These are good vegetables to grow in squares rather than rows. Pinch out the tips to avoid blackfly.

Sowing & Planting

- When the danger of frost has passed, sow sweetcorn (corn) out of doors.
- Sow seeds of cabbages, cauliflowers and Brussel sprouts.
- Plant runner beans out of doors.
- Make a trellis of bamboo canes and plant two seeds at the foot of each cane or plant out beans which have been raised in pots.
- Plant out cabbages and cauliflowers that were sown earlier in seed trays.
- Start thinning early crops such as carrots and spinach, and sow further rows of vegetables like carrots and lettuce to ensure a succession of crops into the autumn.
- Sow French beans (green beans).
- Plan and plant out a herb garden or herb pot.

Above: A formal country house garden may provide ideas on setting out a herb garden, although a less rigid, more natural style is much more popular now than it was in the 19th century.

A Pot of Herbs

If you are short of space, grow your herbs in pots.

1 Here a small bay tree is planted in the centre of a pot.

2 Smaller herbs are then planted around the edge.

Hints & Tips

- An alternative to putting straw around strawberries is to lay strips of black polythene (sheets of black plastic) on the beds and cut slits for the plants.
- Make a mound of compost and sow courgettes (zucchini) and marrows on the top so that the plants can trail down giving the vegetables more room.
- Pinching out the tops of broad beans (fava beans) after flowering helps to prevent blackfly. The tops can be cooked and make a delicious vegetable dish.
- Plant mint in a bucket or large flower pot sunk into the herb bed to stop it from spreading.

Shown here are vegetables grown in a 1.2-m (4-ft) bed system. Many vegetables grow better in squares than in the more traditional rows, particularly broad beans (fava beans) and sweetcorn (corn).

THE GREENHOUSE

Now is the time to apply a summer wash to your greenhouse to shade the plants from the sun. Make sure there is planty of ventilation.

Old earthenware pots stacked in rows. In Edwardian times garden boys would spend much of their time cleaning and sterilizing such for reuse.

- Plant greenhouse tomatoes, cucumbers and peppers in growing bags (pots or boxes).
- Feed potted plants and seedlings regularly.
- Prick out (thin) and pot on late-sown bedding plants.
- Take leaf cuttings of saintpaulias and streptocarpus.
- Prune your greenhouse vine and thin the grapes if there are too many bunches.
- Gradually stop watering bulbs of amaryllis (hippeastrum) and *Cyclamen persicum* as the leaves die down.

SUMMER

I know a bank whereon the wild thyme blows,
Where oxlips and the nodding violet grows
Quite over-canopied with luscious woodbine,
With sweet-musk, roses and with eglantine ...

(*William Shakespeare* A Midsummer Night's Dream)

EARLY SUMMER

THE FLOWER GARDEN

This is the time of year when much of the garden looks at its best, flowers in the herbaceous border open and the first roses begin to bloom.

CARE & PROPAGATION

- Prune shrubs after flowering, cutting out any weak shoots. Among the shrubs which should be treated in this way are philadelphus, weigela, diervilla and lilac.
- Disbud lilac bushes to prevent them becoming overcrowded.
- Prune pyracantha and chaenomeles at the end of the period to keep the plants in shape and encourage the formation of flowering spurs.
- Spray roses if they show signs of disease and dead-head them as the flowers die.
- Pull out suckers of roses, lilac and plum trees. Don't cut them away as this will encourage them to grow more vigorously than before.
- Layer azaleas and rhododendrons.
- Propagate clematis by layering.

Left: You can buy pergola arches and use them to great effect in most gardens. Roses and clematis are often planted in combination and will climb quickly.

- Cut back spent flowers in the rock garden to keep them in shape, and take cuttings if you want to increase your stock.
- Cut back hardy geraniums when they have finished flowering to encourage further blooms later in the year.
- Mow and feed the lawn.

SOWING & PLANTING

- Plant out the summer bedding plants in position: pelargoniums, petunias, antirrhinums, sweet williams and scented stocks.
- Sow seeds of hardy biennial plants, particularly next year's wallflowers, if this has not already been done.

Above: Here the lovely laburnum forms a golden pathway in early summer sun.

Right: A sheltered garden with the lawn surrounded by mature shrubs and herbaceous plants.

Above: A town garden surrounded by a trellis fence supporting roses and ivy, with Campanula carpatica *at the front.*
Left: A dazzling display of azaleas.

Summer Tubs and Pots

1 Prepare your tub. Place a taller plant in the centre, such as this osteospermum.

2 Plant low-growing plants around the edge. Scatter on a decorative mulch, then water.

Hints & Tips

- When dead-heading roses cut the flowers off to the nearest flower bud; further flowers will be produced from this point. Don't cut them right back as this weakens the plant.
- Dead-head all bedding plants regularly as this will encourage further flowering through the season.
- Water the garden if there is a prolonged dry spell and remember that it is better to give plants one good soaking a week or every ten days than a light sprinkling each evening.

THE KITCHEN GARDEN

The main task for the kitchen gardener at this time of year is to protect the fruit from birds, squirrels and mice, otherwise the whole crop may be lost.

CARE & PROPAGATION

- Summer-prune fruit trees grown against walls towards the end of the period: shorten the side shoots to six buds of the current year's growth.
- Spray fruit against aphids and leaf curl.
- Check straw around the strawberries and see that all your fruit is securely netted against birds.
- Thin out all seeds sown earlier in the year, especially carrots, beetroot, parsnips and turnips.

SOWING & PLANTING

- Plant out cabbages, broccoli, calabrese and Brussels sprouts in position if this has not been done before.
- Plant out winter vegetables: leeks, winter greens and celery.
- Pick the first peas when young, especially the mangetout (snow peas) or sugar snap peas where the whole pod is cooked and eaten.
- Dig up a few early potatoes to give yourself a treat.

A lovely traditional walled vegetable garden with espaliered and cordoned fruit trees and a row of runner beans which have been immaculately prepared.

Right: Vegetable gardens can be beautiful too, as is this one where melons are grown in an almost ornamental way.

Hints & Tips

- Be more ruthless about thinning seeds than you think necessary. This will give the vegetables the best chance to grow.
- Cover vegetables with protective netting or fleece to keep off the birds.

THE GREENHOUSE

Old-fashioned greenhouses require constant maintenance but they remain the envy of all gardeners who don't have one.

- Feed potted plants regularly, and keep watering.
- Start to feed indoor tomatoes when the first truss (cluster) has set. Feed about every two weeks.
- Pot up and pot on (transfer) all seedlings as necessary.
- Check root balls and divide congested pot plants.

A greenhouse like this is as much a display as a well-stocked border. If your plants become too numerous give them to friends as presents.

Mid Summer

The Flower Garden

Now is the time when the gardener can relax and enjoy the summer and the garden. Many flowers are at their best and the roses are in full bloom.

A triumphal arch of roses climbs up a trellis and creates a wonderful abundance of flowers.

Right: A pond surrounded by astilbes and ornamental grasses. Water is an attractive feature in any garden.

Care & Propagation

- Dead-head roses.
- Prune rambling roses when they have finished flowering.
- Many shrubs can be propagated by softwood or semi-ripe cuttings taken in summer. Prepare a special cutting bed in a cold frame in the kitchen garden and use this to root your cuttings.
- Disbud early-flowering chrysanthemums.
- Keep dead-heading all plants in the herbaceous border to prevent seeds forming and encourage further flowering.
- Continue to feed and apply weed-killer to your lawn.
- Trim hedges of yew, beech, holly, hazel and hornbeam.

Sowing & Planting

- Sow seeds of hardy perennial plants.
- Plant bulbs of colchicum, autumn-flowering crocus, hardy cyclamen and *Amaryllis belladonna*.

Garden seats are a good addition to any garden. They don't have to be in such a grand setting as here to make just as good an impression.

Hints & Tips

- The importance of pruning rambling roses applies especially to the true ramblers such as the "wichuriana" hybrids and the "banksian" roses. All these flower on growth made the previous year – as opposed to hybrid tea and floribunda roses which flower on growth made in the same year. A good book on pruning will give exact details.
- Among the shrubs that can be propagated by softwood or semi-ripe cuttings are: abutilon, aucuba, berberis (in early autumn), buddleia, callistemon, calluna (heather), ceanothus, ceratostigma, chaenomeles, choisya, cistus (rock roses), cotoneaster, cytisus (broom), daphne, deutzia, elaeagnus, escallonia, euonymus, forsythia, fuchsia, garrya, genista, hebe, hibiscus, hydrangea, hypericum, jasmine, kerria (jew's mallow), lavender, lavatera, lonicera (honeysuckle), olearia (daisy bush), philadelphus, photinia, pieris, potentilla, pyracantha, ribes (flowering currant), rosemary, rubus (flowering bramble), santolina (cotton lavender), sarcococca, skimmia, spiraea, symphoricarpos (snowberry), syringa (lilac), thyme, vaccinium, most viburnums and weigela. Use hormone rooting powder and keep the cuttings moist and well drained.
- Hedges should be trimmed when they become untidy. With those shrubs that are naturally bushy at the base it is usually sufficient to trim them in mid to late summer and again in mid autumn.
- Privet, hawthorn, forsythia and lonicera hedges will require more frequent trimming throughout the summer to keep them in shape.
- If you plant a privet hedge remember to cut it back hard for the first two years as this will encourage the plant to shoot from the base.

Taking Semi-ripe Cuttings

1 Choose shoots that are almost fully grown except for the soft tip.

2 Strip the lower leaves, leaving a short length of stem to insert into the soil.

3 Dip the end of the cutting into water and then into a hormone rooting powder. It is best to put the cuttings in a cold frame or propagator, but they will root outside. Keep moist.

Above: This old garden chair may have seen better days, but it makes a foil for the geraniums and alliums planted around it.

Earthenware pots make a very stylish touch to a garden and are a feature in themselves.

THE KITCHEN GARDEN

Take care to prune your fruit bushes, and enjoy one of the real delights of the kitchen garden by digging some early potatoes when they are very small.

Care & Propagation

- Summer-prune fruit trees. Shorten the side shoots of apple, pear, cherry and plum trees to six leaves of the base.
- Prune back laterals on gooseberry bushes so that you can pick the fruit more easily.
- Cut back unwanted laterals on red and white currant bushes to allow light on to the fruit.
- Sow seeds of spring cabbage to plant out in the autumn.
- Earth up celery and leeks.

Harvesting

- Lift early potatoes. Dig over the soil and replant with winter greens or perpetual spinach (spinach beet).
- Lift shallots when the leaves have turned yellow and store them in a cool dry place.

Hints & Tips

~ Lift potatoes on a dry day and leave them in the open air for three or four hours for the skins to harden. Don't leave them any longer than a day or they will go green.

~ Tidy up the compost heap and turn it over to ensure even decomposition.

~ Continue your war on the weeds in your garden.

A lovely crop of summer strawberries. "Doubtless God could have made a better berry, but doubtless God never did." Isaak Walton, Compleat Angler.

THE GREENHOUSE

Dedicated gardeners use their greenhouses the whole year, but for the average gardener the main crop is the wonderful tomatoes grown in the summer.

- If you grow arum lilies in the greenhouse put them out of doors when the flower spathes are over and bring them in again in the autumn.
- Pot on (transfer to pots) any seeds sown in the spring.
- Feed potted plants.
- Remove side shoots from tomatoes and take off any leaves that turn yellow. Stop them when they have set five trusses (clusters) of fruit.
- Pinch out the growing tip of aubergines (eggplants) and allow only one fruit per shoot.
- Spray when pests and diseases appear.

Left and above: Greenhouses can be used for a number of gardening tasks. Professional and dedicated amateur gardeners use them to propagate house plants and exotic climbers. You have to be prepared, however, to keep your greenhouse properly heated if you want to grow plants of the type shown here.

LATE SUMMER

THE FLOWER GARDEN

The end of summer is brightened by the summer bulbs which are now at their best, particularly the lovely agapanthus lilies, which can be easily grown in tubs.

- Take cuttings of hardy fuchsias to increase your stock or raise plants which you can exchange with other gardeners.
- Sow seeds of hardy annuals out of doors to flower early next summer.
- Take cuttings of evergreen shrubs. Keep them in pots of sandy soil in a shaded cold frame for four to five weeks before planting on.
- Take cuttings of pelargoniums, dip in rooting powder and plant.
- Plant your spring bulbs now: Madonna lily (*Lilium candidum*), *Amaryllis belladonna*, hardy cyclamen, snowdrops, crocus, squill, winter aconites and Glory of the Snow (chionodoxa).

Old garden seats make a focal point in any garden, however big or small. Here pots surround the seat and ground cover plants grow in between the bricks.

A rather formal, but still attractive, effect is created by these topiary formations standing in old terracotta pots.

Hints & Tips

- Water hardy fuchsias each evening – this encourages flowering.
- Hardy annuals that can be sown out of doors include cornflowers, poppies, love-in-a-mist (nigella), larkspur and scabious.
- When you take pelargonium cuttings leave them in the air overnight to form a callous at the base, then dip them in hormone rooting powder and pot them up. This prevents the stems from rotting.
- Agapanthus lilies grow well in pots, as do hostas. This is a good way to enjoy hostas, which are particularly vulnerable to slugs when grown in borders.

THE KITCHEN GARDEN

This is the time of year to start enjoying the young vegetables. Nothing bought from a shop will ever taste so good.

CARE & PROPAGATION

- Examine your plum trees and cut down and burn any which show signs of silver leaf to prevent the disease spreading.
- Make a new strawberry bed by planting up runners from this year's plants.
- Prune blackcurrant bushes when fruiting is over.
- Spray runner beans with water each evening to encourage the flowers to set and make sure that the plants have plenty of moisture.
- Guard against attacks by caterpillars, which can destroy most type of cabbages and greens almost overnight.

HARVESTING

- Pick the early apples as they ripen and eat them straight away. They will not keep.
- Gather raspberries and currants. Cut down the old raspberry canes (vines) when they have finished fruiting, leaving four to five new shoots to each plant.
- Pick and enjoy the vegetables as they ripen.
- Lift onions as they become ripe.

A well-kept kitchen garden with vegetables ready for picking and the first flowers appearing on the runner beans. Water these each evening to help set the flowers.

Hints & Tips

- Blackcurrants fruit on growth made the previous year, so on mature bushes cut out two or three old branches completely and take other fruiting branches down to vigorous side shoots.
- Lift onions during a dry period and allow them to dry outside before plaiting (braiding) them up into onion strings.
- Feed the whole kitchen garden with liquid fertilizer.

THE GREENHOUSE

There is little to do in the greenhouse in late summer, other than feeding, watering and sowing.

Fuschias and begonias are just some of the flowers in this well-stocked greenhouse display.

- Sow spring-flowering plants such as cyclamen and schizanthus.
- Continue to feed tomatoes every two weeks.
- Continue to feed potted plants every two weeks.
- Plant prepared hyacinth bulbs for early flowering when these become available.

AUTUMN

Season of mists and mellow fruitfulness,
Close bosom-friend of the maturing sun;
Conspiring with him how to load and bless
With fruit the vines that round the thatch-eaves run.

(John Keats "Ode to Autumn")

EARLY AUTUMN

THE FLOWER GARDEN

As the nights get shorter the leaves on the trees start to change colour. Autumn is the time of the year to plant new trees and shrubs.

CARE & PROPAGATION

- Prepare the site of a new lawn so it is ready for sowing.
- Tie in new shoots of climbing and rambling roses.
- Check on the cuttings taken earlier in the year and remove any that have failed to strike (sprout).
- Lift and divide border irises if they have not flowered well.
- Cut the leaves of the winter-flowering iris (*Iris unguicularis* syn. *I. stylosa*) in half. This encourages the production of more flowers.
- Take cuttings of summer bedding plants for propagation.
- Take cuttings of plants like fuchsias, violas, pelargoniums and penstemons.
- When summer bedding plants start to die back clear the beds, fork them over (till the soil) and prepare them for bedding plants such as winter-flowering pansies.

SOWING & PLANTING

- Sow grass seed to repair worn patches in the lawn. Fork over (aerate) the soil and add a small amount of general fertilizer.
- Sow sweet peas in pots and place them in a cold frame.
- Plant evergreen shrubs and trees at the end of the period.
- It is not too late to plant early spring-flowering bulbs – winter aconites (they are treated as bulbs although they are really tuberous plants), snowdrops, the Siberian squill, chionodoxa, fritillaries, grape hyacinths (muscari), anemones and crocuses.
- Plant daffodils and narcissus, as they will flower better if they are planted now rather than later.
- Plant lily bulbs if they are available now.
- Plant rock garden plants. Now is a good time of the year to make a rock garden if you want to establish one.
- Plant border carnations and pinks.

Pergolas and other frames are easy to construct using larch poles. They were often seen in old-fashioned gardens covered with climbing roses and honeysuckle.

*Above: The fabulous and unmistakeable red leaves of a Japanese maple (*Acer palmatum*) in autumn.*

Hints & Tips

- Prepare the site of a new lawn carefully; make sure that the soil is level and that you have access to a roller. If the lawn germinates correctly, you will be able to mow it very lightly once or twice before the end of the year, and it should be well established by the following year.
- Take time to admire the berries on the flowering trees like rowans and hawthorn.
- Start sweeping up the leaves as they fall. Don't wait until the trees are bare.
- Lift iris rhizomes carefully, pull them apart and replant the outside pieces with a shoot attached. The rhizomes should be only half covered with soil, as they need to be baked by the sun if they are to produce the best flowers. They prefer deeply dug soil which has been enriched by well-rotted manure or compost, and the ground will need a sprinkling of lime every three years.
- Snowdrops are often tricky to establish from bulbs and do better if they are planted "in the green" when they have finished flowering in spring. Many suppliers sell them this way.
- Cuttings of the hardier plants are best rooted in a cold frame which you can cover with matting in very cold weather, but cuttings of pelargoniums need a minimum temperature of 7°C (45°F) to keep them safe over the winter months.

THE KITCHEN GARDEN & GREENHOUSE

Main crop potatoes can be harvested and stored as can apples, carrots, turnips and beetroot.

CARE & PROPAGATION

- If frost threatens, cover lettuces with cloches to prolong the growing season.
- Grease-band fruit trees to prevent winter moths from crawling up into the branches.
- Protect outdoor tomatoes if the weather turns cold.
- Plant spring cabbage.
- Earth up leeks and celery.
- Blanch endives by covering them with a pot or slate.
- If you want you can sow a green fertilizer crop, such as clover, to dig in to the garden next spring.

HARVESTING

- Lift onions as they ripen.
- Lift and store main crop potatoes, carrots, turnips and beetroot (beets).
- Pick outdoor tomatoes as they ripen.
- Continue to harvest French beans.

Right: An old-fashioned wheelbarrow piled with produce as it might appear in a Dutch still-life painting. It is often possible to give away any surplus vegetables at this time of year to neighbours who don't have a kitchen garden of their own.

THE GREENHOUSE

- Check that your greenhouse heater is working properly.
- Clean off the greenhouse summer shading washes ready for winter.
- Bring in chrysanthemums that are to flower later in the autumn. It is a good idea to check all the plants thoroughly for any signs of disease or pests, especially mildew.
- Take inside all the house and greenhouse plants that have spent the summer out of doors.
- Plant hyacinth bulbs that are to flower indoors in the winter and place them in the dark for six weeks or so until the root systems have formed.
- Repot cacti if required.
- Sow spring-flowering plants such as cyclamen, schizanthus and exacum.

Dig up your potatoes on a dry day and leave them exposed to the air for three or four hours for the skin to harden, before you store them.

Hints & Tips

- Don't forget that tomatoes ripen with warmth not sunshine, so if you want you can pick all your tomatoes when they are green, store them carefully in a cool dry place, and then bring them up to the kitchen to ripen as you need to use them. If you still have a glut, make some chutney.
- Beware of wasps when picking fruit and buy some antihistamine tablets from the chemist in case anyone gets stung and has an allergic reaction. It is really quite important to remember this as in extreme cases wasp stings can be fatal unless they are treated immediately.

Mid Autumn

The Flower Garden

For many the middle of autumn is the start of the gardening year, new plans are made while the colour on the trees is complemented by the autumn flowers.

Amelanchier laevis, *"The Snowy Mespilus", is one of the best trees for any small garden, with its white flowers in the spring and wonderful autumn colour.*

Care & Propagation

- Lay a new lawn from turf or sow seed on to a prepared site.
- Apply an autumn dressing of combined weedkiller and fertilizer to the lawn.
- Shift any shrubs that may require moving, but only when there has been a good amount of rain and the soil is damp.
- Divide large herbaceous plants.
- Take cuttings of evergreen shrubs.
- Take cuttings of roses.
- Lift and store all the summer-flowering tuberous plants such as gladioli, dahlias and begonias.
- If you have a pond, now is the time to thin out the plants, divide those which have grown too large and remove the tender aquatic plants to the greenhouse.
- Collect up and compost leaves as they fall.
- Prune rambler and climbing roses.

Now is the time of year to lift gladioli corms and bring them indoors. Label all bulbs carefully.

Planting

- Plant conifers and evergreens.
- Plant evergreen hedges. Dig a good trench and keep the plants moist for several weeks after planting.
- Plant clematis and climbing shrubs such as *Hydrangea petiolaris*, wisteria, ornamental vines, summer jasmine, honeysuckle and ivy. Soak them well before planting.
- Plant out any summer biennials such as foxgloves which you have raised from seed and plant pansies and primulas for a winter and spring display.
- Plant wallflowers in position ready to flower the following summer.
- Plant spring bulbs such as daffodils and tulips. Remember to plant spring pots and window-boxes too.

Ceratostigma plumbaginoides *in autumn. These plants are grown specifically for their lovely blue flowers and autumn foliage.*

Raking up leaves can be a long, hard task; little and often is a good rule.

Hints & Tips

- When moving shrubs, dig out a large hole all around the plant and take as much earth with the roots as possible. Puddle (water) them in well to give the roots a chance to establish.
- Take care when planting evergreens to prepare the holes in advance and don't leave bare roots exposed to the air if this can be avoided. Don't cover the top roots by more than 5–7.5 cm (2–3 in) of soil and water them well after planting. Mulch the following spring with well-rotted compost or leaf mould.
- It is preferable to plant fairly small evergreens as they will establish themselves better and ultimately make better plants.
- When planting clematis, dig a good-sized hole 60 x 45 cm (24 x 18 in) and fill it with good soil enriched by decayed manure and mortar rubble. Wash all the soil away from the roots of your plant and carefully spread them out in the hole before back-filling. The plant will flower much better than if you just put it in a hole in the normal way.
- Plant all bulbs deeply – at least two and a half times the depth of the bulb – and feed when flowering is finished.
- Put tender aquatic plants in a plastic container with a little water and some soil, and keep them in the greenhouse for the winter.
- Skim fallen leaves which have landed in the pond with a butterfly or pond net.

THE KITCHEN GARDEN

Start clearing the vegetables in preparation for the autumn digging. Add compost and manure to improve the fertility and quality of the soil.

CARE & PROPAGATION

- Take cuttings of fruit bushes.
- Prune raspberries, blackberries, blackcurrants, loganberries and Morello cherries.
- Plant spring cabbages.
- Thin late-sown lettuces.
- Cut down asparagus stalks when they have died down.
- Clean and disinfect the greenhouse and remove the summer wash ready for the winter.
- Start clearing and winter digging, especially if you have heavy soil.
- Take in some summer bedding plants to overwinter. These will provide plenty of cuttings for the following year.
- Pot up prepared bulbs for flowering indoors in the winter: hyacinths, daffodils, narcissi and crocuses are good choices.
- Plant any fruit trees and bushes and put grease bands on apple trees.

HARVESTING

- Pick and store apples and pears.
- Lift potatoes, carrots and beetroot (beets) and store in a cool dry place. Parsnips should be left in the ground and dug as required.

Onions and potatoes laid out to dry before being brought indoors. Obviously, it is essential to do this on a dry day.

Above: A magnificent giant pumpkin of the kind that is so often used as a lantern at Halloween, or for the traditional, seasonal pumpkin pie.

Hints & Tips

- If you don't have proper fruit racks leave apples and pears in a dry place for a week for the skins to dry and then wrap them in paper and keep them in boxes in the cellar or a cool shed.
- The best way to store carrots and beetroot (beets) is to set them between layers of sand or peaty compost. This helps to preserve the flavour for longer.

LATE AUTUMN

THE FLOWER GARDEN

It is a good idea to have some plants in your garden grown specially for their autumn colour. Acers and fothergillas are particularly rewarding.

Lichens cover a stone urn on a limestone balustrade.

CARE & PROPAGATION

- This is the best season to plant trees, roses and shrubs.
- Apply weedkiller to the lawn.
- The world is divided into those who trim and tidy their herbaceous borders in late autumn and those who leave this until early spring. If you leave everything in place until the spring the dead foliage will provide some protection for the less hardy plants, while the patterns of frost on the dead leaves give pleasure to the eye in the winter.
- Take cuttings of shrubs and insert them in a prepared trench.
- Remove the water pump from the pond for the winter.
- Protect any tender plants against early frosts.
- Dig up and move any plants in the herbaceous border which are in the wrong position.

Hints & Tips

- Generally, the longer the time between planting and flowering in all shrubs and trees, the better the final result will be.
- Stake any standard trees or shrubs when planting to prevent them from being broken, damaged or loosened in the soil by the wind.
- When planting any new plant make sure that you label it properly. Otherwise you may well forget not only what the plant is but also where it is.
- When taking cuttings of shrubs prepare a narrow trench and scatter sand at the bottom. Cuttings should be about 23 cm (9 in) long and inserted 15 cm (6 in) into the ground. Leave them undisturbed for a year.

THE KITCHEN GARDEN & GREENHOUSE

Collect all the autumn leaves to make leaf mould or to add to your garden compost. If you shred them they will break down more quickly. If you heat your greenhouse, check the thermometer and ensure that it is properly ventilated on fine days.

- Dig over any vacant ground and add compost. Double-dig any part of the kitchen garden where you intend to grow any special crops.
- Lime heavy (clay) soils if required.
- Start pruning fruit trees and spray them against pests.
- Sow seeds of broad beans (fava beans).

Taking a heel cutting from an elaeagnus. A heel of the old wood is taken with the shoot.

Hardwood cuttings are planted in a trench with added grit for drainage.

GREENHOUSE

- Clean the greenhouse and insulate it against the winter. Use bubble wrap held in place with pins or special fasteners.
- Bring in chrysanthemums and tender fuchsias.
- Check your minimum temperature with a maximum/minimum thermometer.
- Ventilate the greenhouse on sunny days.
- Take chrysanthemum cuttings when the plants have finished flowering.
- Prune the greenhouse vine, if you have one.

Hints & Tips

- Collect and compost leaves. If you have a rotary mower this will collect all the leaves easily and is quicker and less back-breaking than raking them up into piles.
- Burn or dispose of all garden rubbish: don't leave it piled up to harbour pests and diseases.
- When you dig make no attempt to break the soil down. Leave it in rough clods, exposing as large an area as possible. The action of rain and frost helps to break down the soil and makes cultivation easier the following spring.
- Except for those which flower during the winter, gradually reduce the amount of water you give your plants.
- Bring in any spring-flowering bulbs you have placed out of doors in pots.

WINTER

That time of year thou may'st in me behold
When yellow leaves, or none, or few, do hang
Upon those boughs which shake against the cold,
Bare ruin'd choirs, where late the sweet birds sang.

(William Shakespeare "Sonnet 73")

Early Winter

The Flower Garden

All gardens should have plants that flower in the short days of winter, such as witch hazel, winter jasmine, winter heathers, winter iris and hellebores.

- Top-dress the lawn with sand, if you garden on heavy soil, to improve the drainage and quality of the grass.
- Check any bulbs and tubers you have in store and remove any that show signs of rot.
- Finish off all the tasks left over from the last two months.
- It is not too late to plant bare-root trees and shrubs if weather and soil conditions permit. You can even take cuttings from shrubs if there is a mild spell.
- Sweep up the last of the fallen leaves.
- Clear up the edges of the garden and burn or throw away all rubbish.
- Sow seeds of rock plants and put them out of doors in boxes in a bed of ash.
- Prune roses. Opinions differ as to the best season to do this but you can opt to prune in the winter when they are dormant.

Hints & Tips

~ If the ground is very wet and you need to plant shrubs or trees, put some dry soil or compost around the roots.

Above: Sowing seeds into cellular seed trays for planting out in the summer.
Left: It is a good idea to protect tender plants in winter; here a bay tree is being covered with tubular fleece.

THE KITCHEN GARDEN

Start pruning your fruit trees and make sure that apricots are pruned when they are dormant.

Collect up garden rubbish and burn it in small, manageable fires. Make sure nothing toxic or inorganic is in the pile before you set the fire alight.

- Continue winter digging and add compost or lime.
- It is an old English country custom to plant shallots on the shortest day of the year.
- Take cuttings of fruit bushes if this has not been done before.
- Lift leeks and parsnips as required.
- Start forcing rhubarb.
- Continue pruning fruit trees, particularly apricot trees which must be pruned at this time of year.

Hints & Tips

- Test your soil before adding lime and apply carefully, following the manufacturer's instructions.
- Collect up your garden canes (stakes) and stand the ends in wood preservative for a day.
- Check over all your garden tools. Get shears and secateurs (pruners) sharpened professionally.
- Check all your greenhouse plants once a week and pick off dead or dying leaves before rot starts.
- Water plants sparingly; better to be too dry than too wet.
- Check winter-flowering bulbs and bring them into the light when they are 3–5 cm (1–2 in) tall.

MID WINTER

THE FLOWER GARDEN

Even in mid winter many of the early flowering shrubs like Viburnum tinus *and* V. farreri *come into bloom as the first bulbs start to flower.*

- Order seeds, summer bulbs and plants for next season.
- Replan your garden and draw out the design of any new beds on paper to ensure that you get the plants in the right place.
- Knock any heavy settled snow off trees, shrubs and hedges as it can damage branches and spoil the shape of the bush.
- See that all half-hardy shrubs and plants are fully protected if the weather is cold.
- Take root cuttings of plants such as acanthus, echinops, gaillardia, phlox and *Primula denticulata.*

Hints & Tips

- Wrap plants in polythene (plastic) to protect them from frost or cover them in straw.
- If you have a bed exposed to strong east winds erect a temporary fence with stakes and attach sacking (burlap) or polythene (plastic) along the back. This is an enormous help in preventing shrubs from being damaged by frost.
- If there is a prolonged freeze-up break the ice on the pond.

Left: Delicate winter pansies, even more lovely with a dusting of snow.

Above: A heavy fall of snow can easily break or damage branches, so knock it off before it becomes too heavy.

THE KITCHEN GARDEN & GREENHOUSE

A kitchen garden on a cold frosty day in mid winter is a daunting prospect when you have to pick the Brussel sprouts for Sunday lunch, but it is also full of promise for the new year. Use the long evenings of winter to begin planning your next planting season.

- Finish pruning and spraying fruit trees.
- Force seakale (Swiss chard).
- Sow broad beans (fava beans) under cloches in mild parts of the country.

GREENHOUSE

- If you can provide enough heat you can start sowing seeds in trays. You can sow vegetables such as carrots and lettuce and also flowers such as sweet peas, gloxinias, antirrhinums, dahlias, begonias and hollyhocks.
- Take cuttings of chrysanthemums.

Hints & Tips

- Plan your kitchen garden for the coming year and make sure that the crops are properly rotated.
- If you have a hot bed you can sow early lettuces, radishes and cauliflowers.
- Don't sow too many seeds if your greenhouse isn't heated and you cannot provide a bright enough position in which to grow the seedlings on.
- If you have a propagator that you can keep indoors on a bright window ledge, this is probably the best way to start seeds at this time of year.

If you plant seeds in pots they will need pricking out so that just one seedling remains.

Viburnum tinus *is one of the best winter-flowering shrubs with dark green leaves and small fragrant pink-ish white flowers.*

LATE WINTER

THE FLOWER GARDEN

Gardening at this time of year depends entirely on the weather. Don't be lulled by a mild spell into planting seeds out of doors as the frosts will usually return.

- Start clearing up the herbaceous border and fill in any gaps. Add a mulch to the border when you have finished clearing up.
- Plant climbers. Plant out any shrubs or trees that you were unable to plant the previous autumn.
- Renovate garden paths.
- Prune roses if you did not do so earlier in the year.
- Prune clematis, buddleia, *Hydrangea paniculata* and *Spiraea japonica.*
- Plant summer-flowering bulbs: gladioli, galtonia and lilies.
- Dig out a new herbaceous border if you have planned one.
- Create a rock garden, or a pool for water lilies.

Choisya ternata *"Sundance" that has suffered frost damage. The species plant is hardier.*

Pots of herbs covered in snow. Herbs usually come to no harm in winter, but some of the Mediterranean herbs such as rosemary may need a little protection.

Hints & Tips

- Admire the cyclamen, almond blossom and the other flowers that come out at this time of year.
- If the weather is wet and you garden on heavy clay don't try to cultivate your beds or kitchen garden – you will do more harm than good. Leave them until the soil is drier. You can always catch up when the weather improves.

THE KITCHEN GARDEN & GREENHOUSE

One of the joys of a kitchen garden is digging it over on mild days at the end of winter. Better exercise than jogging and you have a nice expanse of brown earth at the end. Now is the time to tidy and organize your greenhouse and make ready to sow the first seeds of the New Year.

- Plant broad beans (fava beans) if this was not done in late autumn.
- Finish digging and add manure to the soil.
- Chit (sprout) seed potatoes.
- Put cloches or sheets of clear polythene (plastic) over the beds to start warming up the soil.
- Cut down autumn-fruiting raspberries.
- Lift and separate old clumps of rhubarb.
- Plant first early potatoes if you live in a mild climate and plant shallots and Jerusalem artichokes.
- Spray peaches and nectarines against leaf-curl.

GREENHOUSE

- Take chrysanthemum cuttings.
- Pot up chrysanthemum cuttings taken earlier.
- Start sowing seeds of annuals and hardy border perennials.
- Take cuttings of any summer bedding plants that you have kept over winter in the greenhouse.

Above: If you remove leaves from Brussel sprouts the heads will achieve better growth.

Below: The epitome of winter – a swede (rutabage) poking its leaves through the snow.

Picture Acknowledgements

Above: A common garden shed adorned with flowers.

Photographs in the book were taken by:
Peter Anderson, Michelle Garrett, Jacqui Hurst, Lucy Mason
and Debbie Patterson.

Other pictures were supplied by Peter McHoy for the following pages:
6/7, 8, 11, 13, 24, 33, 42, 43, 44/45, 47, 49, 50, 51, 52, 53, 54 (top),
55, 56/57, 58, 59, 60, 61, 62 and 63.